MathFlare

Name: _______________________

Class: ___________

Teacher: _______________________

Introduction

As parents and educators, we recognize the pivotal role mathematics plays in shaping a child's academic journey and future success. Yet, the path to mathematical proficiency can often seem daunting, fraught with challenges and complexities. That's where the transformative power of MathFlare Workbooks shine through, illuminating the way forward with clarity, precision, and purpose.

Introducing MathFlare Workbooks – a beacon of guidance, a testament to excellence, and a catalyst for achievement. Crafted with meticulous care and expertise, MathFlare Workbooks stand as paragons of educational excellence, designed to nurture young minds, ignite a passion for learning, and develop a deep-rooted understanding of mathematical concepts.

Picture this: your child eagerly delves into the pages of Mathflare Workbook, greeted by a step-by-step guide illuminated with vivid examples that demystify complex mathematical concepts. With each turn of the page, they embark on a journey of discovery, encountering thoughtfully curated practice questions that reinforce learning and hone problem-solving skills. And when they unveil the answers to those very questions, a sense of accomplishment blossoms within them – a tangible reward for their hard work and dedication.

But MathFlare Workbooks are more than just tools for learning; they are pathways to comprehension, fostering a deep-seated understanding of mathematical concepts through a sequential, logical flow. From fundamental principles to advanced problem-solving strategies, every chapter builds upon the last, ensuring a robust foundation upon which future knowledge can be constructed.

As parents, we yearn for nothing more than to see our children thrive, to witness the spark of inspiration ignited within them as they conquer academic challenges with confidence and poise. MathFlare Workbooks serve as partners in this noble endeavor, offering not just practice questions, but the keys to unlocking a world of opportunity.

And for teachers, MathFlare Workbooks stand as invaluable allies in the quest to cultivate mathematical proficiency in the classroom. With answers readily available, instructors can focus on guiding and nurturing their students, confident in the knowledge that MathFlare Workbooks provide a solid framework upon which to build.

In the pages of MathFlare Workbooks, we find not just the promise of academic excellence, but the seeds of a brighter tomorrow. So let us embrace the power of mathematics, let us champion the journey of learning, and let us pave the way for a generation of young minds poised to shape the world. With MathFlare Workbooks as our guide, the possibilities are infinite, and the future, bright.

Table of Contents

MathFlare
MATH WORKBOOK
Grade 2
Addition Subtraction
Multiplication
Place Value and Expanded Notations
Geometry
Step by Step Guide and Essential Practice with Answers

MathFlare
MATH WORKBOOK
Grade 2-3
Addition Subtraction
Multiplication and Division
Place Value and Expanded Notations
Geometry
Step by Step Guide and Essential Practice with Answers

MathFlare
MATH WORKBOOK
Grade 3
Multiplication and Division
Decimals
Place Value and Expanded Notations
Fractions and Geometry
Step by Step Guide and Essential Practice with Answers

MathFlare
MATH WORKBOOK
Grade 1
Counting and Numbers
Addition and Subtraction
Place Value and Expanded Notations
Understanding Time
Step by Step Guide and Essential Practice with Answers

MathFlare
MATH WORKBOOK
Grade 1-2
Counting and Numbers
Addition and Subtraction
Place Value and Expanded Notations
Understanding Time
Step by Step Guide and Essential Practice with Answers

MathFlare
MATH WORKBOOK
Grade 3-4
Addition Subtraction
Multiplication Division
Place Value and Expanded Notations
Fractions and Geometry
Step by Step Guide and Essential Practice with Answers

MathFlare
MATH WORKBOOK
Grade 4
Addition Subtraction
Multiplication Division
Place Value and Expanded Notations
Fractions and Geometry
Step by Step Guide and Essential Practice with Answers

MathFlare
MATH WORKBOOK
Grade 4-5
Multiplication Division
Place Value and Expanded Notations
Fractions and Geometry
Unit Conversion
Step by Step Guide and Essential Practice with Answers

MathFlare
Grade 5
MATH WORKBOOK
Step by Step Guide and Essential Practice with Answers
Multiplication Division
Place Value and Expanded Notations
Fractions and Geometry
Unit Conversion
MathFlare Publishing

MathFlare
Grade 5-6
MATH WORKBOOK
Step by Step Guide and Essential Practice with Answers
Multiplication Division
Place Value and Expanded Notations
Fractions and Geometry
Units and Statistics
MathFlare Publishing

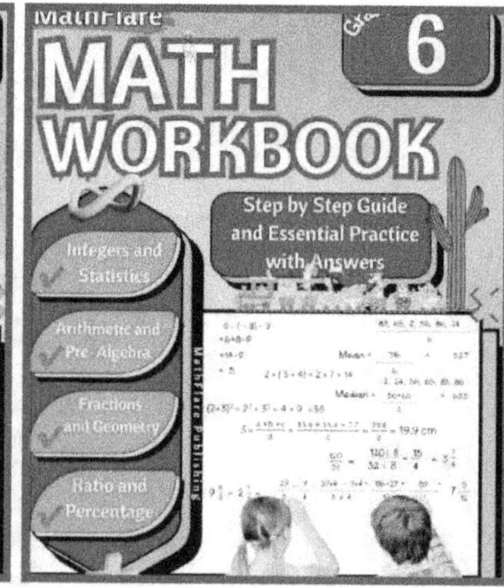
MathFlare
Grade 6
MATH WORKBOOK
Step by Step Guide and Essential Practice with Answers
Integers and Statistics
Arithmetic and Pre-Algebra
Fractions and Geometry
Ratio and Percentage
MathFlare Publishing

MathFlare
Grade 6-7
MATH WORKBOOK
Step by Step Guide and Essential Practice with Answers
Arithmetic and Pre-Algebra
Ratio, Percent Proportion
Geometry
Statistics
MathFlare Publishing

MathFlare
Grade 7
MATH WORKBOOK
Step by Step Guide and Essential Practice with Answers
Pre-Algebra
Ratio, Percent Proportion
Geometry
Statistics
MathFlare Publishing

MathFlare
Grade 7-8
MATH WORKBOOK
Step by Step Guide and Essential Practice with Answers
Pre-Algebra
Ratio, Percent Proportion
Geometry and Cartesian Plane
Statistics
MathFlare Publishing

MathFlare
Grade 8-9
MATH WORKBOOK
Step by Step Guide and Essential Practice with Answers
Pre-Algebra
Ratio, Proportion and Percentage
Linear Equations
Geometry and Cartesian Plane
MathFlare Publishing

MathFlare
Grade 8
MATH WORKBOOK
Step by Step Guide and Essential Practice with Answers
Pre-Algebra
Percentage
Linear Equations
Geometry
MathFlare Publishing

Factors and Multiples

Factors and multiples are two fundamental concepts in mathematics.

Factors:

- Factors are numbers that divide another number without leaving a remainder.

- For example, the factors of 12 are 1, 2, 3, 4, 6, and 12 because these numbers can divide 12 evenly.

- Factors always come in pairs, except for perfect squares.

Multiples:

- Multiples are the result of multiplying a number by an integer.

- For example, the multiples of 3 are 3, 6, 9, 12, 15, and so on because these numbers are obtained by multiplying 3 by 1, 2, 3, 4, 5, and so on.

- Every number has an infinite number of multiples.

Every factor of a number is a divisor of that number, and every multiple of a number is divisible by that number.

Let's solve some problems:

Factors of **44**

2, 4, 11, 22

Multiples of **77**

77, 154, 231, 308, 385

Least Common Multiple (LCM)

The Lowest Common Multiple (LCM) of two or more numbers is the smallest multiple that is divisible by each of the numbers.

There are several methods to find the LCM; however, we will focus on only two:

Listing Multiples: List the multiples of each number until you find a common multiple. For example:

$$
\begin{array}{r|l}
8 & 8,\ 16,\ 24,\ 32,\ 40,\ 48,\ 56 \\
\hline
7 & 7,\ 14,\ 21,\ 28,\ 35,\ 42,\ 49,\ 56
\end{array}
\quad , \text{ LCM} = \underline{56}
$$

Division Method: Divide each number with the smallest prime number that divides at least one of the numbers evenly. The product of all the divisors and quotients is the LCM. For example:

$$
\begin{array}{c|cc}
2 & 7 & 8 \\
\hline
2 & 7 & 4 \\
\hline
2 & 7 & 2 \\
\hline
7 & 7 & 1 \\
\hline
& 1 & 1
\end{array}
$$

$$\text{LCM} = 2 \times 2 \times 2 \times 7 = \underline{56}$$

Both methods have their advantages. For big numbers, using the division way is usually faster. But if we are working with smaller numbers or like seeing patterns, listing multiples might make more sense.

Prime Numbers

A prime number is a natural number greater than 1 that has no positive divisors other than 1 and itself.

Rules for Prime Numbers:

1. Prime numbers are greater than 1.

2. Prime numbers have only two distinct positive divisors: 1 and the number itself.

3. Prime numbers are not divisible by any other number except 1 and themselves.

4. 2 is the only even prime number.

Methods for Identifying Prime Numbers:

1. Trial Division: Check divisibility by all numbers up to the square root of the number.

2. Sieve of Eratosthenes: Generate a list of prime numbers up to a certain limit by eliminating multiples of prime numbers.

3. Using Prime Factorization: Factorize the number into its prime factors.

For Example: Let's analyze a few numbers to determine if they are prime or not:

Number	Is Prime?
7	Yes
8	No (divisible by 2)
19	Yes
65	No (divisible by 5)
221	No (divisible by 13)

<u>Greatest Common Factors</u>

The Greatest Common Factor (GCF), also known as the Greatest Common Divisor (GCD), of two or more numbers is the largest number that divides each of the numbers without leaving a remainder. It is the greatest number that is a common factor of the given numbers.

There are two main methods to find the GCF:

- Prime Factorization,
- Using Factors.

Let's find GCF of 44, and 33 using factors:

- List all the factors of each number:

  Factors of 44: 1, 2, 4, 11, 22, 44 Factors of 33: 1, 3, 11, 33

- Identify and chose the common factors:

  The common factor between 44 and 33 is 11.

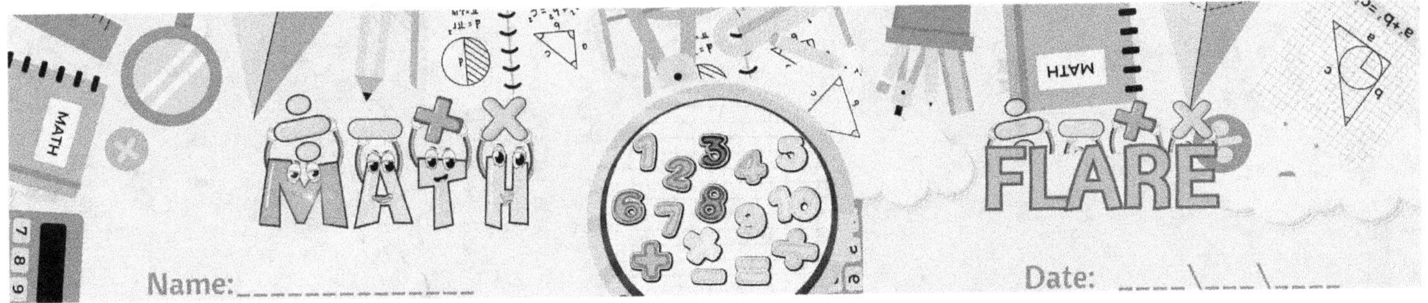

Factors

1. 49 ____

2. 63 ____

3. 6 ____

4. 261 ____

5. 16 ____

6. 48 ____

7. 51 ____

8. 27 ____

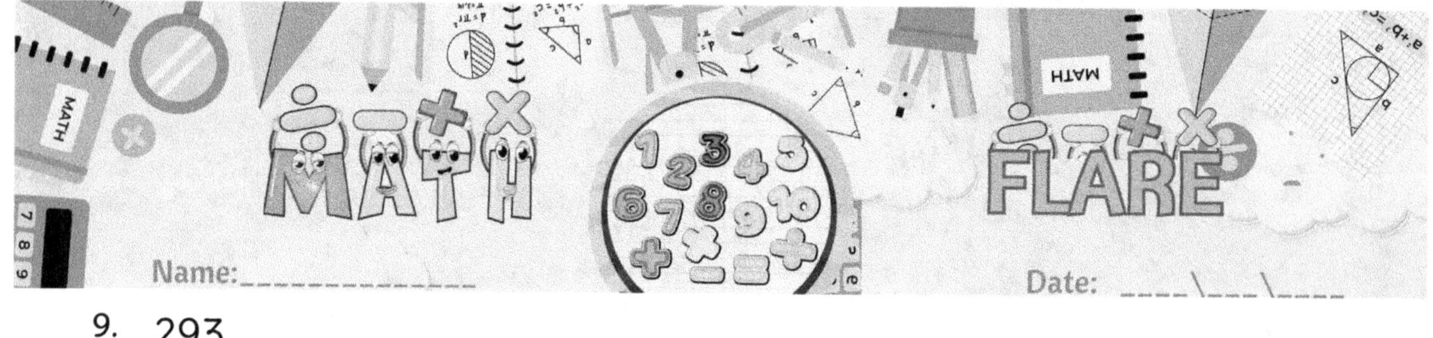

9. 293 _______________________________

10. 461 _______________________________

11. 93 _______________________________

12. 432 _______________________________

13. 2 _______________________________

14. 337 _______________________________

15. 64 _______________________________

16. 4 _______________________________

17. 95 ____

18. 287 ____

19. 14 ____

20. 7 ____

21. 5 ____

22. 10 ____

23. 8 ____

24. 9 ____

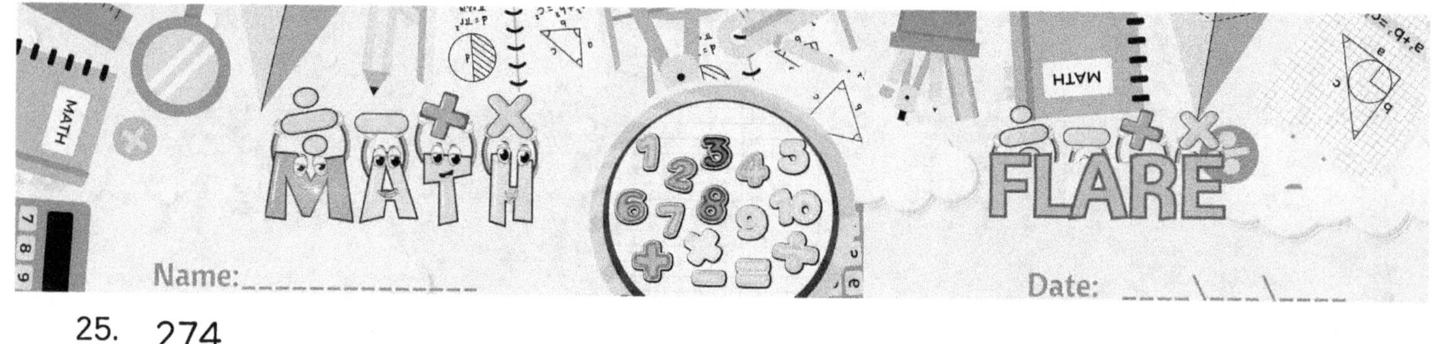

25. 274 _______________________________

26. 321 _______________________________

27. 89 _______________________________

28. 131 _______________________________

29. 437 _______________________________

30. 117 _______________________________

31. 342 _______________________________

32. 24 _______________________________

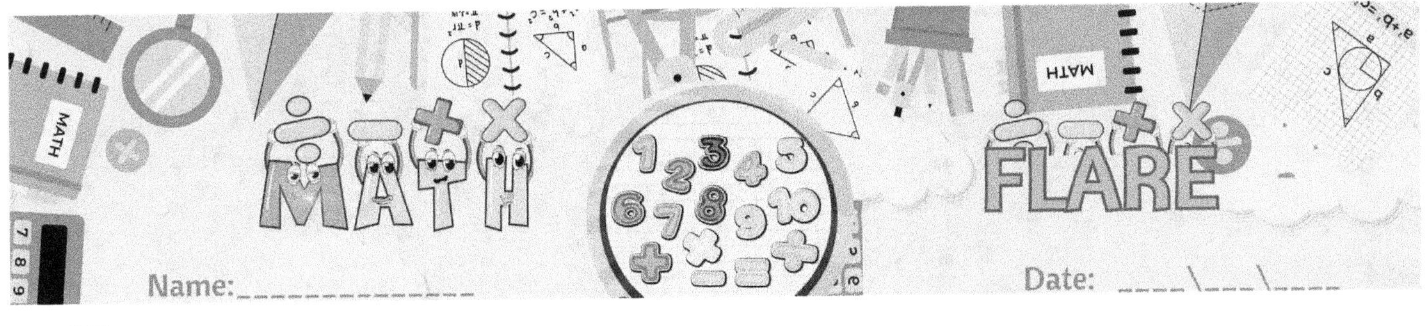

33. 392 ______________________________

34. 22 ______________________________

35. 107 ______________________________

36. 165 ______________________________

37. 11 ______________________________

38. 111 ______________________________

39. 60 ______________________________

40. 99 ______________________________

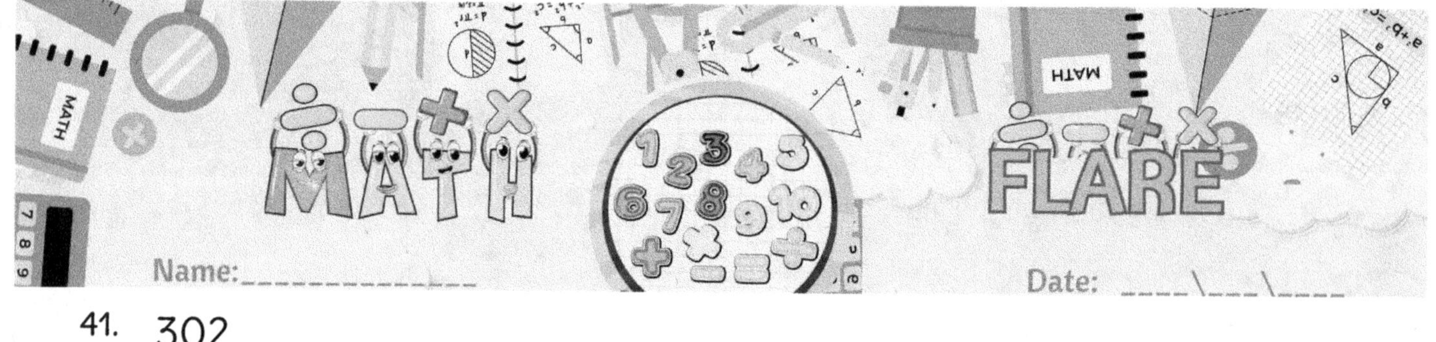

41. 302 ____

42. 490 ____

43. 20 ____

44. 1 ____

45. 43 ____

46. 228 ____

47. 3 ____

48. 303 ____

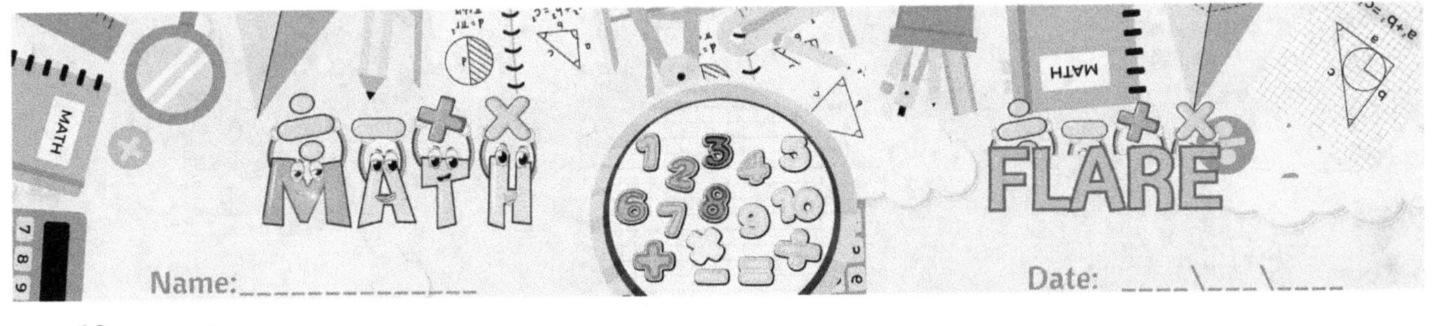

49. 315 ____

50. 396 ____

51. 38 ____

52. 12 ____

53. 72 ____

54. 41 ____

55. 265 ____

56. 330 ____

57. 192 ____

58. 466 ____

59. 37 ____

60. 54 ____

61. 100 ____

62. 238 ____

63. 309 ____

64. 46 ____

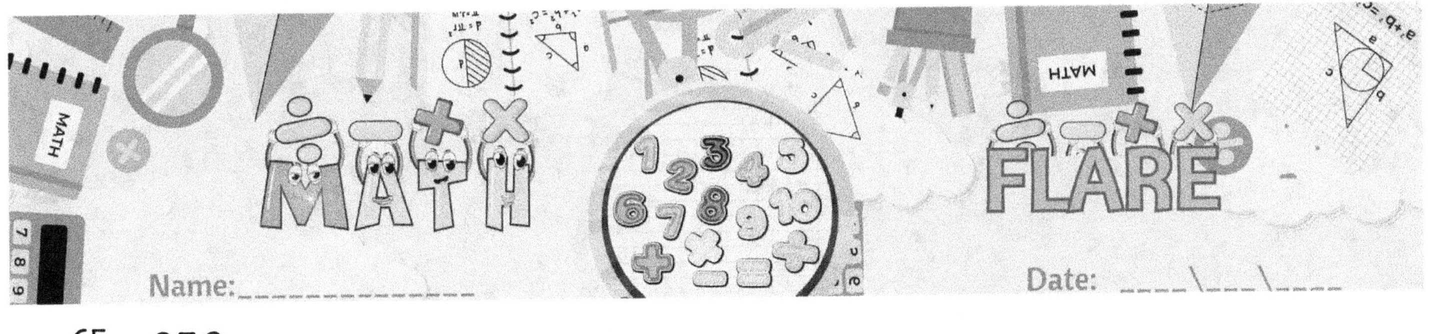

65. 250 _______________________

66. 374 _______________________

67. 242 _______________________

68. 258 _______________________

69. 376 _______________________

70. 86 _______________________

71. 57 _______________________

72. 132 _______________________

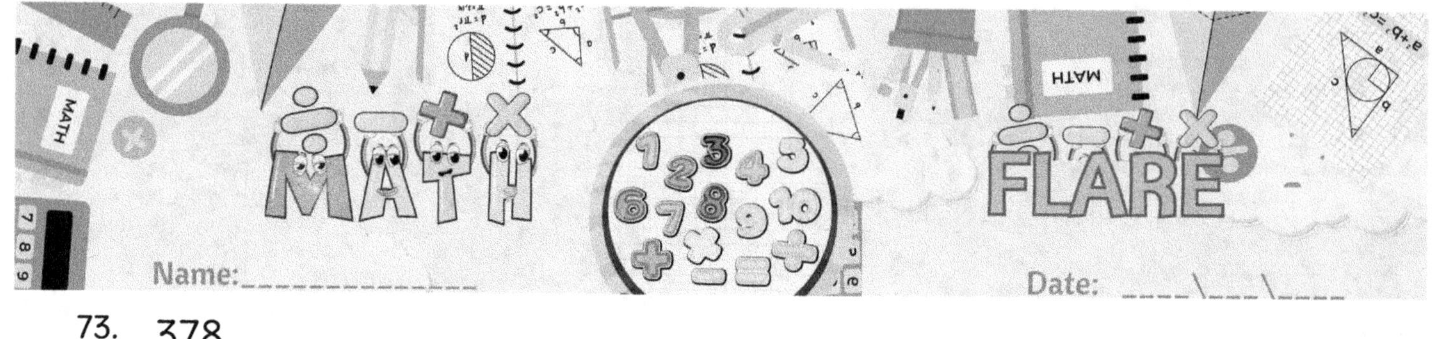

73. 378 ___________________________

74. 69 ___________________________

75. 334 ___________________________

76. 168 ___________________________

77. 82 ___________________________

78. 413 ___________________________

79. 92 ___________________________

80. 138 ___________________________

Prime Numbers

Is the number prime? List the prime factors for each number.

81. 1 = _______________________

82. 8 = _______________________

83. 65 = _______________________

84. 221 = _______________________

85. 19 = _______________________

86. 7 = _______________________

87. 192 = _______________________

88. 35 = _______________________

89. 145 = _______________________

90. 500 = _______________________

91. 90 = _______________________

92. 44 = _______________________

93. 9 = _______________________

94. 454 = _______________________

95. 82 = _______________

96. 187 = _______________

97. 196 = _______________

98. 81 = _______________

99. 208 = _______________

100. 4 = _______________

101. 33 = _______________

102. 443 = _______________

103. 18 = _______________

104. 5 = _______________

105. 147 = _______________

106. 3 = _______________

107. 310 = _______________

108. 6 = _______________

109. 2 = _______________

110. 42 = _______________

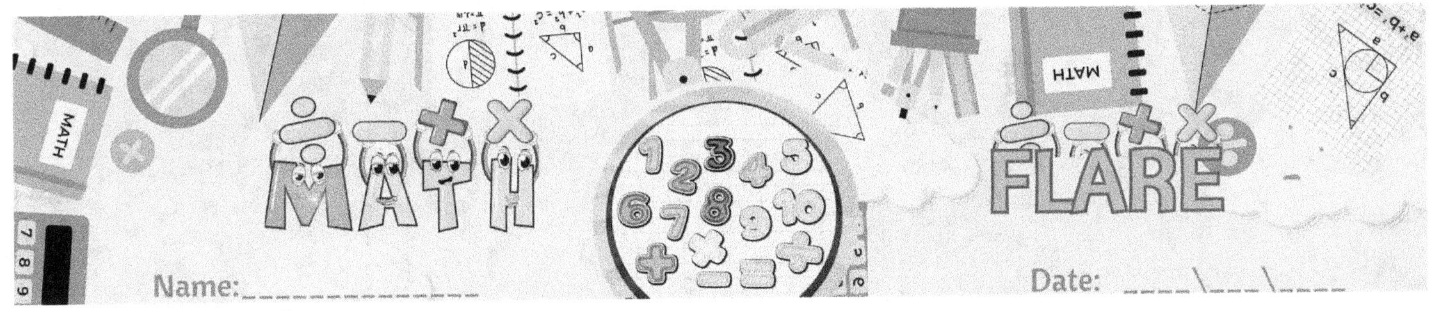

111. 59 = ________________

112. 375 = ________________

113. 198 = ________________

114. 179 = ________________

115. 273 = ________________

116. 58 = ________________

117. 347 = ________________

118. 87 = ________________

119. 214 = ________________

120. 27 = ________________

121. 61 = ________________

122. 320 = ________________

123. 494 = ________________

124. 425 = ________________

125. 388 = ________________

126. 94 = ________________

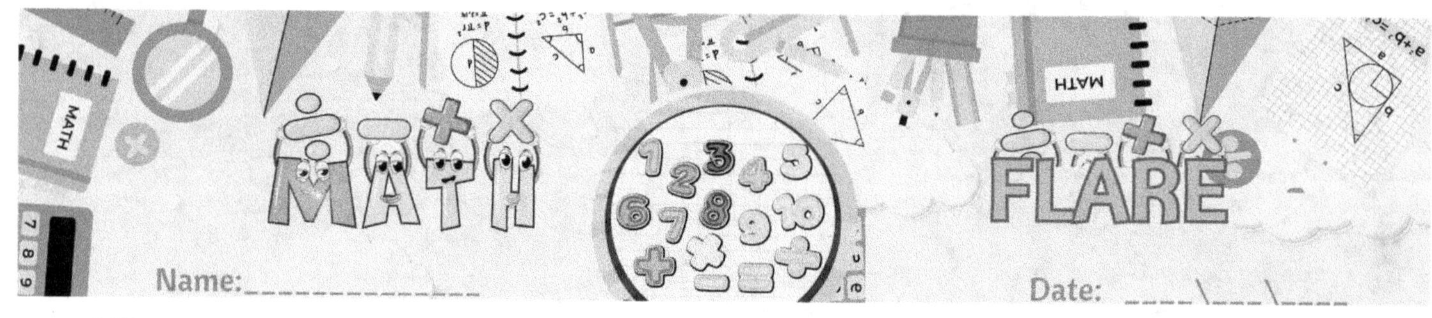

127. 68 = _______________

128. 95 = _______________

129. 105 = _______________

130. 31 = _______________

131. 332 = _______________

132. 292 = _______________

133. 56 = _______________

134. 50 = _______________

135. 298 = _______________

136. 28 = _______________

137. 357 = _______________

138. 64 = _______________

139. 142 = _______________

140. 102 = _______________

141. 93 = _______________

142. 315 = _______________

143. 380 = __________________

144. 23 = __________________

145. 49 = __________________

146. 92 = __________________

147. 62 = __________________

148. 341 = __________________

149. 89 = __________________

150. 25 = __________________

151. 13 = __________________

152. 350 = __________________

153. 253 = __________________

154. 392 = __________________

155. 69 = __________________

156. 328 = __________________

157. 398 = __________________

158. 269 = __________________

Greatest Common Factor

Find the greatest common factor.

159. 252
      432

160. 146
      116

161. 254
      398

162. 268
      364

163. 182
       98

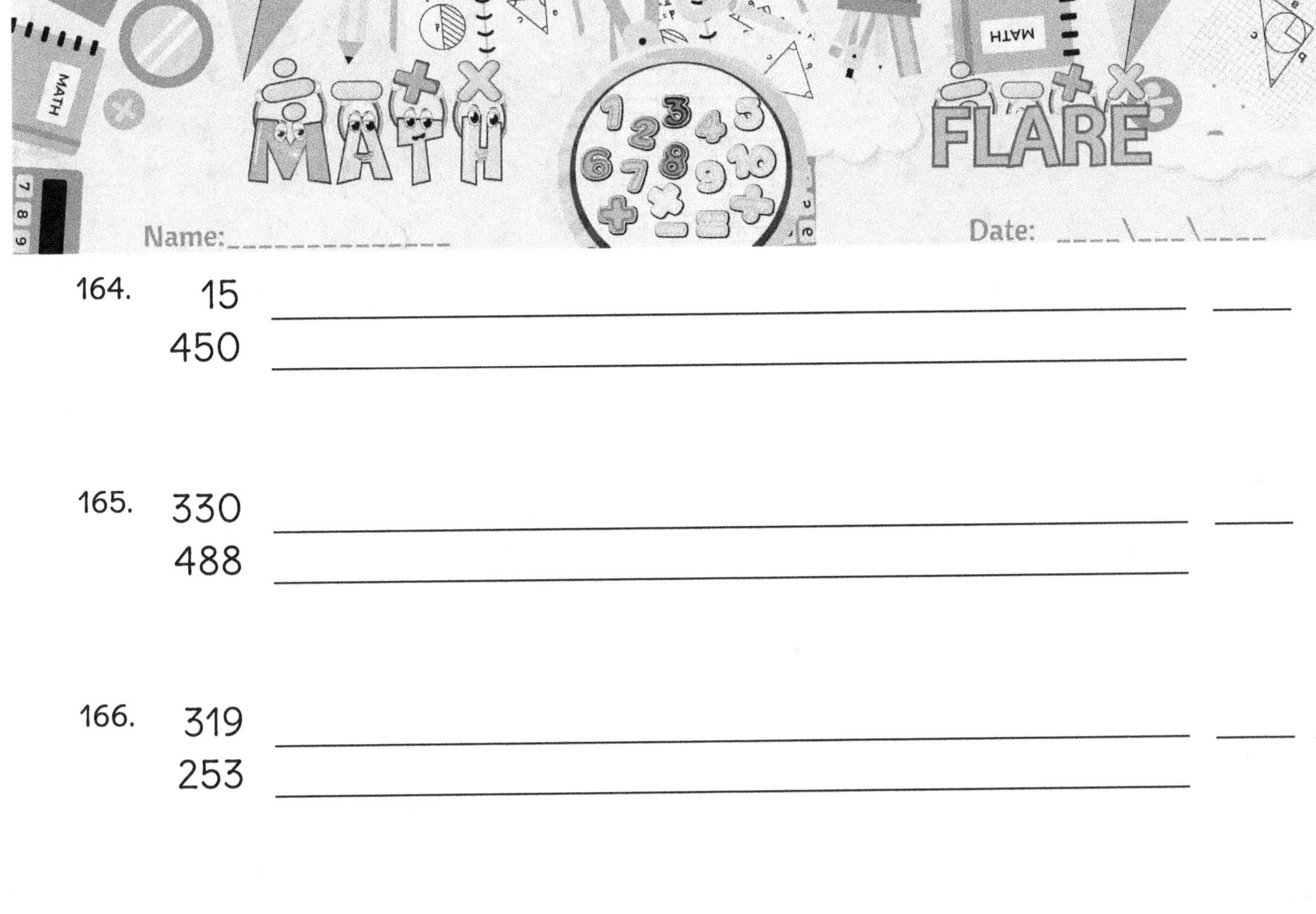

164. 15
      450

165. 330
      488

166. 319
      253

167. 65
      250

168. 355
      205

169. 330
      286

170. 63 _______________________________________ ___
357 _______________________________________

171. 385 _______________________________________ ___
112 _______________________________________

172. 440 _______________________________________ ___
418 _______________________________________

173. 125 _______________________________________ ___
150 _______________________________________

174. 469 _______________________________________ ___
49 _______________________________________

175. 220 _______________________________________ ___
33 _______________________________________

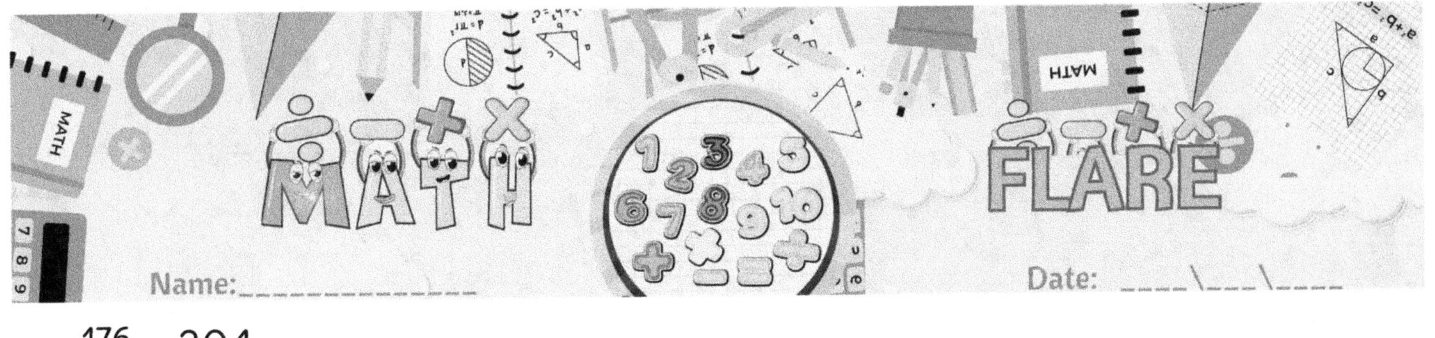

176. 204 __________________________ ____
     426 __________________________

177. 205 __________________________ ____
     265 __________________________

178. 396 __________________________ ____
     186 __________________________

179. 273 __________________________ ____
     411 __________________________

180. 352 __________________________ ____
     450 __________________________

181. 378 __________________________ ____
     441 __________________________

182. 112 _______________________________ ____
      378 _______________________________

183. 480 _______________________________ ____
      255 _______________________________

184. 435 _______________________________ ____
       95 _______________________________

185. 336 _______________________________ ____
      129 _______________________________

186. 252 _______________________________ ____
      126 _______________________________

187. 284 _______________________________ ____
      358 _______________________________

188. 154 _______________________ ___
     484 _______________________

189. 248 _______________________ ___
     176 _______________________

190. 280 _______________________ ___
     275 _______________________

191. 428 _______________________ ___
     120 _______________________

192. 296 _______________________ ___
     344 _______________________

193. 96 _______________________ ___
     94 _______________________

194. 342 _______________________________ ___
     224 _______________________________

195.   4 _______________________________ ___
     460 _______________________________

196. 445 _______________________________ ___
     435 _______________________________

197. 490 _______________________________ ___
      95 _______________________________

198. 444 _______________________________ ___
      70 _______________________________

199. 450 _______________________________ ___
     360 _______________________________

200. 330
198 ___

201. 105
40 ___

202. 68
160 ___

203. 318
441 ___

204. 86
154 ___

205. 330
300 ___

206. 228 _______________________________   ___
      291 _______________________________

207.   74 _______________________________   ___
      484 _______________________________

208.   6 _______________________________   ___
      294 _______________________________

209. 140 _______________________________   ___
      145 _______________________________

210. 344 _______________________________   ___
       14 _______________________________

211.   33 _______________________________   ___
       66 _______________________________

212. 112 _______________________ ___
      343 _______________________

213. 495 _______________________ ___
      418 _______________________

214. 195 _______________________ ___
      126 _______________________

215. 456 _______________________ ___
      416 _______________________

216. 428 _______________________ ___
      118 _______________________

217. 462 _______________________ ___
      99 _______________________

218. 300 _________________________ ___
     358 _________________________

219. 425 _________________________ ___
     95 _________________________

220. 170 _________________________ ___
     426 _________________________

221. 297 _________________________ ___
     473 _________________________

222. 112 _________________________ ___
     54 _________________________

223. 77 _________________________ ___
     209 _________________________

224. 343
231

225. 238
378

226. 420
49

227. 44
216

228. 165
374

229. 115
230

230. 425
      190

231. 143
      319

232. 423
      393

233. 196
      343

234. 484
      341

235. 105
      112

Multiples

236. 2 ____

237. 233 ____

238. 1 ____

239. 200 ____

240. 97 ____

241. 9 ____

242. 76 ____

243. 46 ____

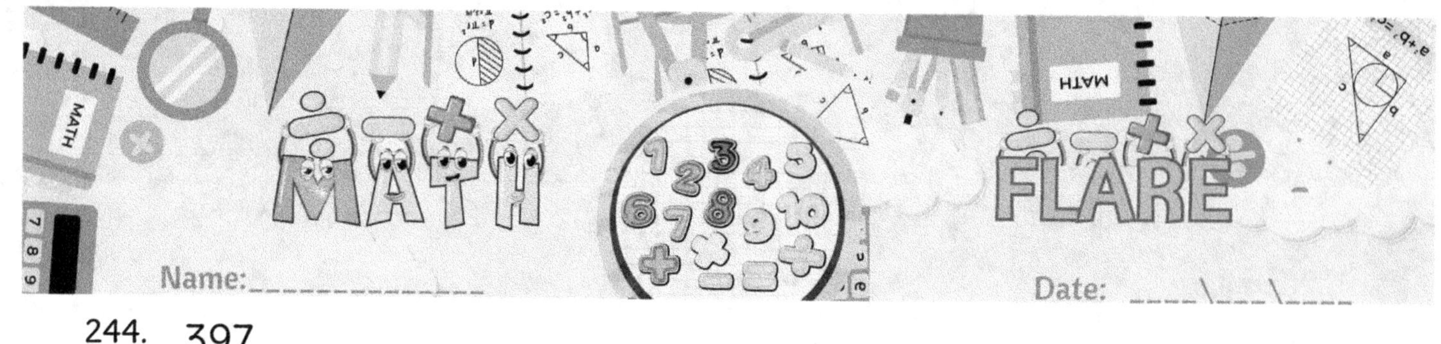

Name: _______________

Date: _______________

244. 397 ____

245. 50 ____

246. 12 ____

247. 7 ____

248. 17 ____

249. 4 ____

250. 56 ____

251. 45 ____

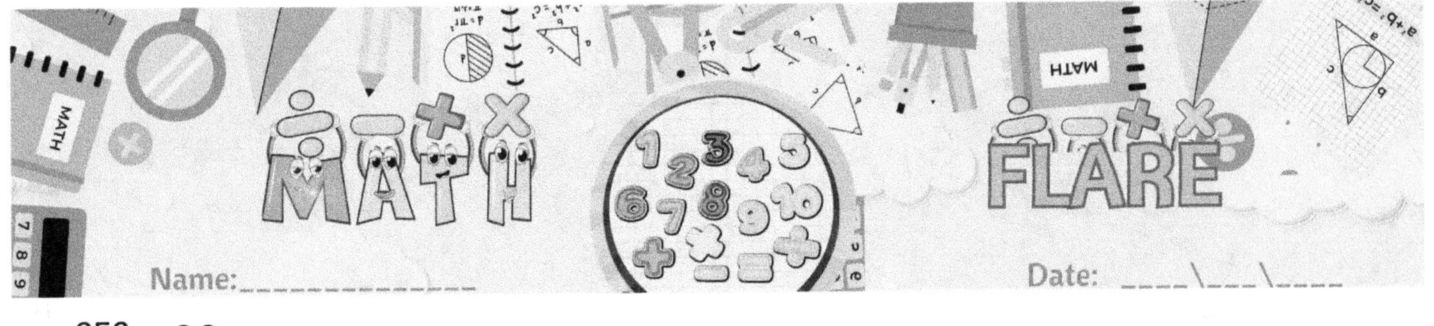

252. 89 _______________________________________

253. 20 _______________________________________

254. 72 _______________________________________

255. 3 _______________________________________

256. 77 _______________________________________

257. 432 _______________________________________

258. 236 _______________________________________

259. 98 _______________________________________

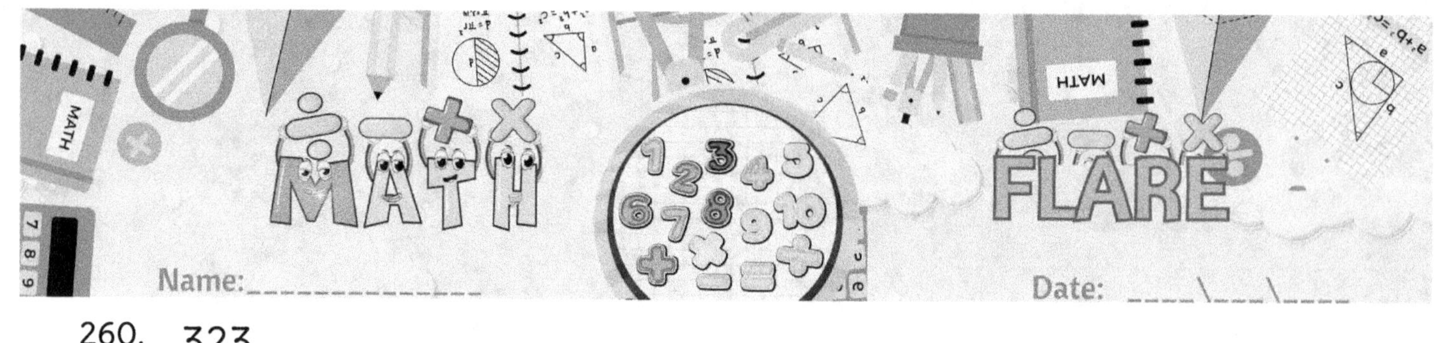

260. 323 _______________________________

261. 383 _______________________________

262. 152 _______________________________

263. 95 _______________________________

264. 219 _______________________________

265. 8 _______________________________

266. 108 _______________________________

267. 265 _______________________________

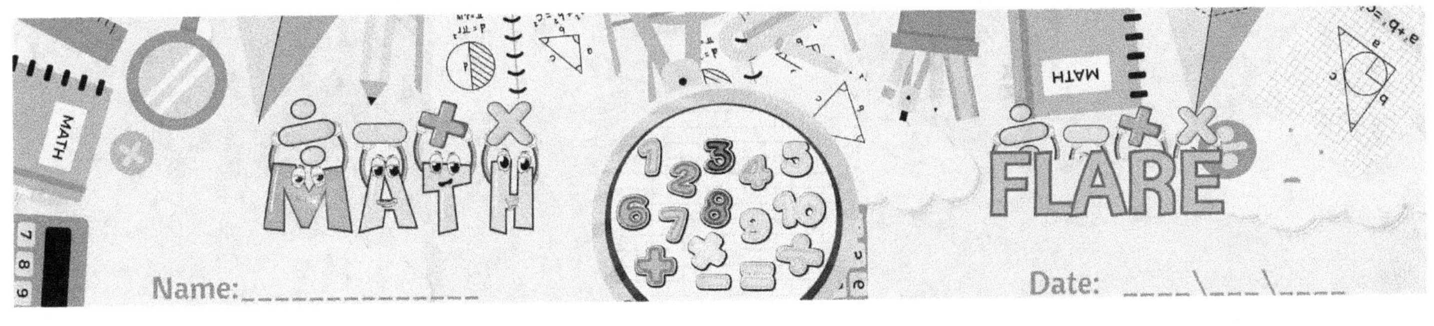

268. 37 ____

269. 444 ____

270. 55 ____

271. 73 ____

272. 297 ____

273. 83 ____

274. 440 ____

275. 47 ____

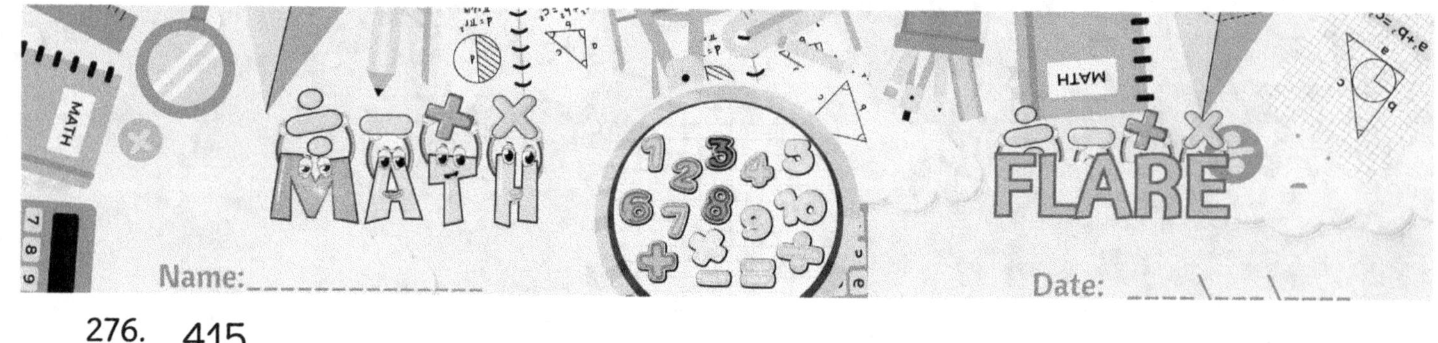

276. 415 __________________________________

277. 346 __________________________________

278. 304 __________________________________

279. 64 __________________________________

280. 214 __________________________________

281. 28 __________________________________

282. 482 __________________________________

283. 121 __________________________________

284. 79 _______________________________

285. 14 _______________________________

286. 368 _______________________________

287. 164 _______________________________

288. 388 _______________________________

289. 62 _______________________________

290. 361 _______________________________

291. 22 _______________________________

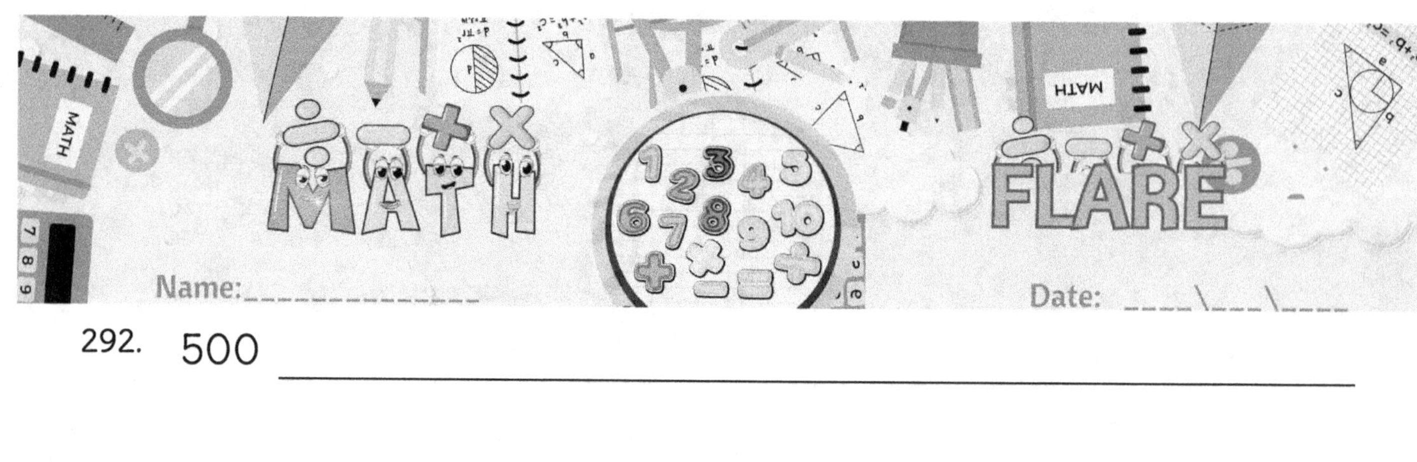

292. 500 ____

293. 96 ____

294. 80 ____

295. 29 ____

296. 30 ____

297. 88 ____

298. 5 ____

299. 422 ____

300. 6 _______________________________________

301. 67 ______________________________________

302. 183 _____________________________________

303. 36 ______________________________________

304. 171 _____________________________________

305. 60 ______________________________________

306. 172 _____________________________________

307. 353 _____________________________________

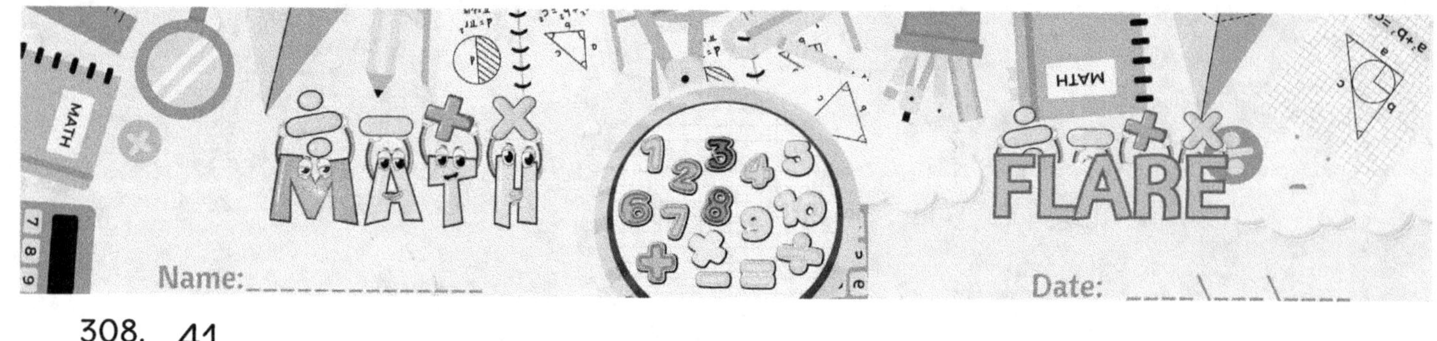

308. 41 ____

309. 364 ____

310. 293 ____

311. 54 ____

312. 33 ____

313. 457 ____

314. 499 ____

315. 400 ____

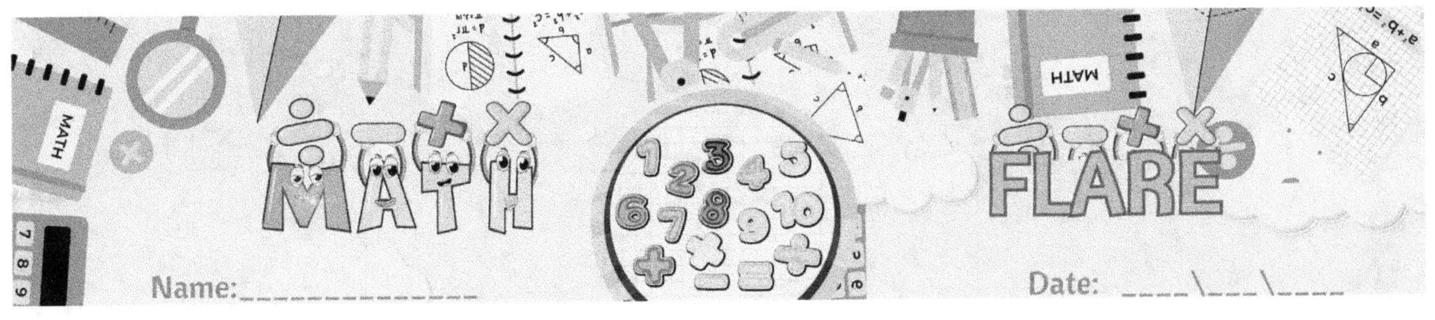

316. 366 ____

317. 487 ____

318. 266 ____

319. 90 ____

320. 403 ____

321. 21 ____

322. 85 ____

323. 426 ____

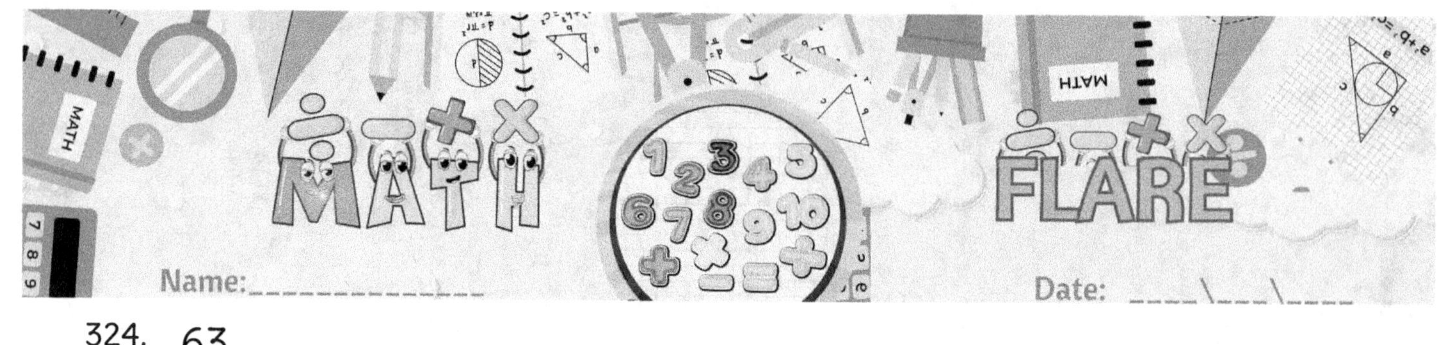

324. 63 ____

325. 132 ____

326. 365 ____

327. 27 ____

328. 39 ____

329. 386 ____

330. 138 ____

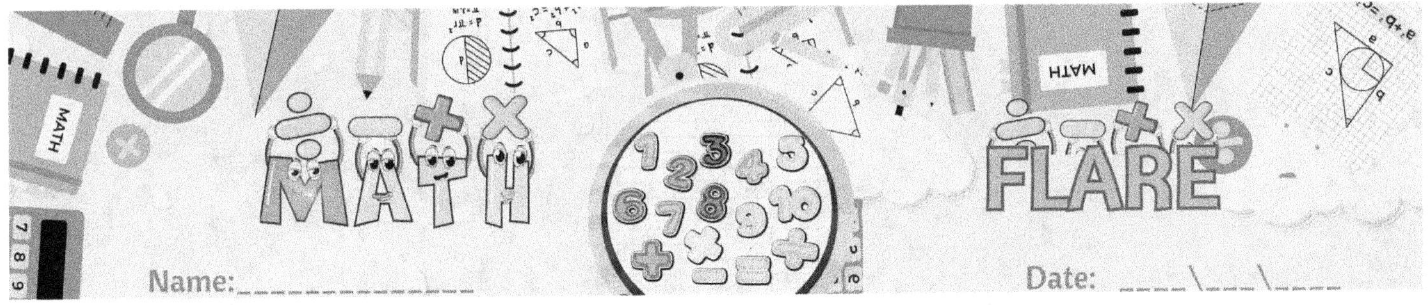

Lowest Common Multiple

Find the lowest common multiple.

331. 3
      421

332. 87
      232

333. 111
      3

334. 391
      9

335. 62
      70

336.   3
       51

337.   474

       480

338.   3
       76

339.   401

       174

340.   9
       3

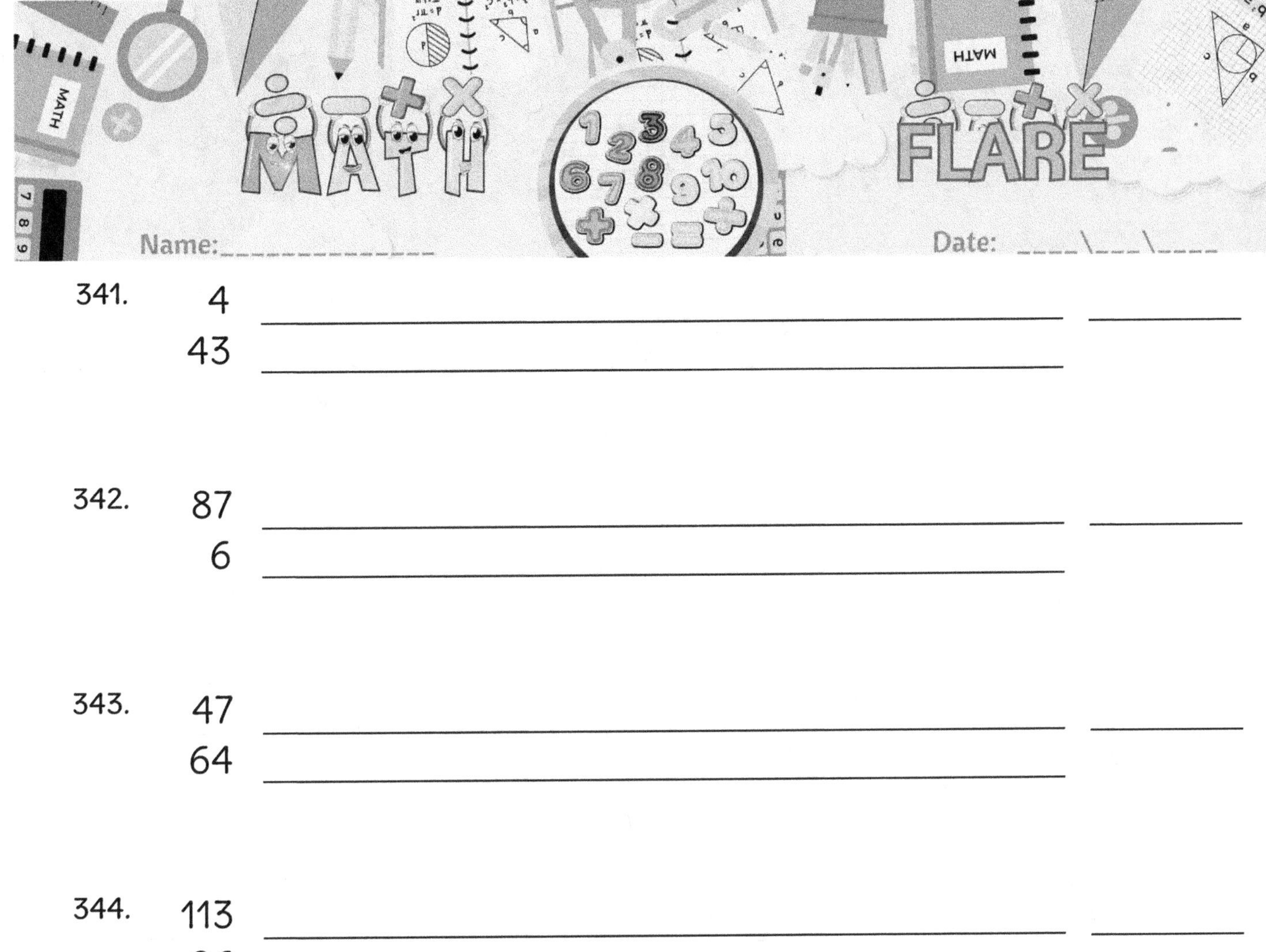

341. 4
      43

342. 87
      6

343. 47
      64

344. 113
      26

345. 34
      97

346. 2
      288

347. 6 ______________________________ ______
      8 ______________________________

348. 33 ______________________________ ______
      6 ______________________________

349. 3 ______________________________ ______
      99 ______________________________

350. 20 ______________________________ ______
      116 ______________________________

351. 162 ______________________________ ______
      81 ______________________________

352. 96 ______________________________ ______
      468 ______________________________

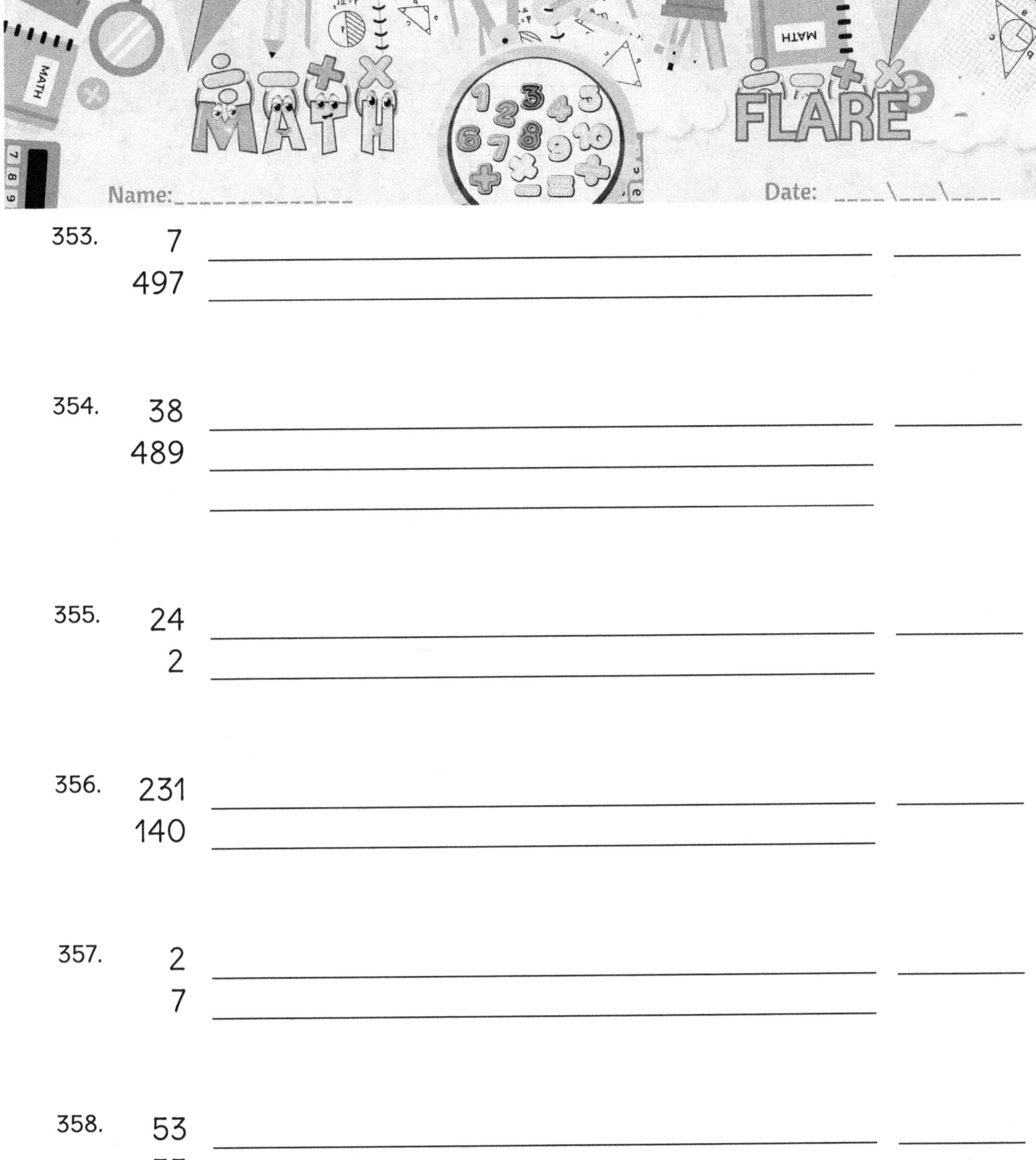

Name: _______________________   Date: ____________

353. 7
      497

354. 38
      489

355. 24
      2

356. 231
      140

357. 2
      7

358. 53
      33

359. 44
      3

360. 25
      180

361. 20
      10

362. 29
      490

363. 7
      45

364. 407
      5

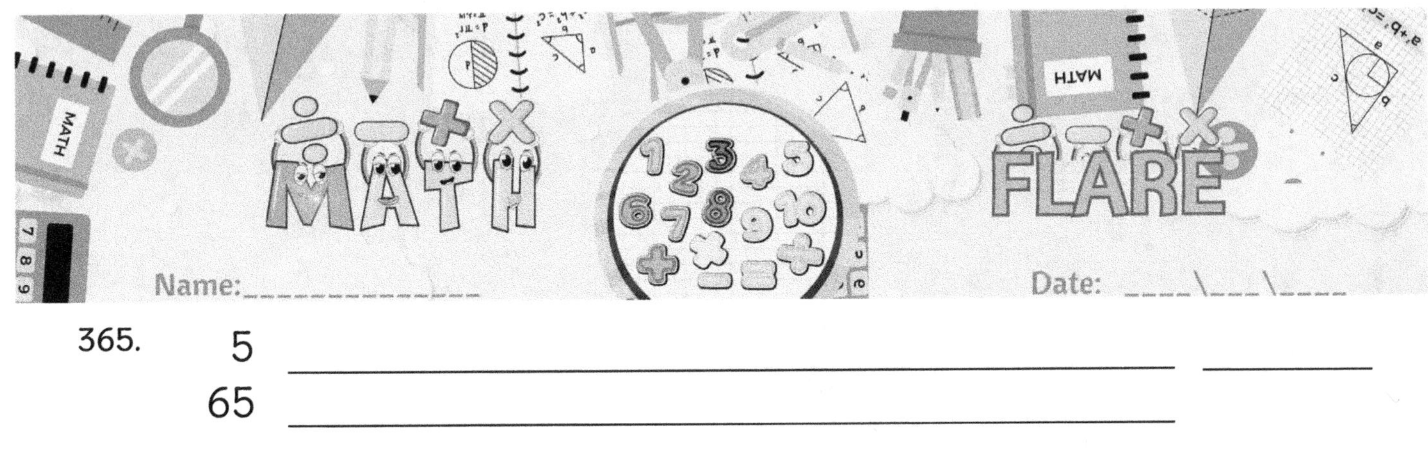

365. 5
      65

366. 26
      80

367. 6
      25

368. 7
      26

369. 11
      73

370. 460
      98

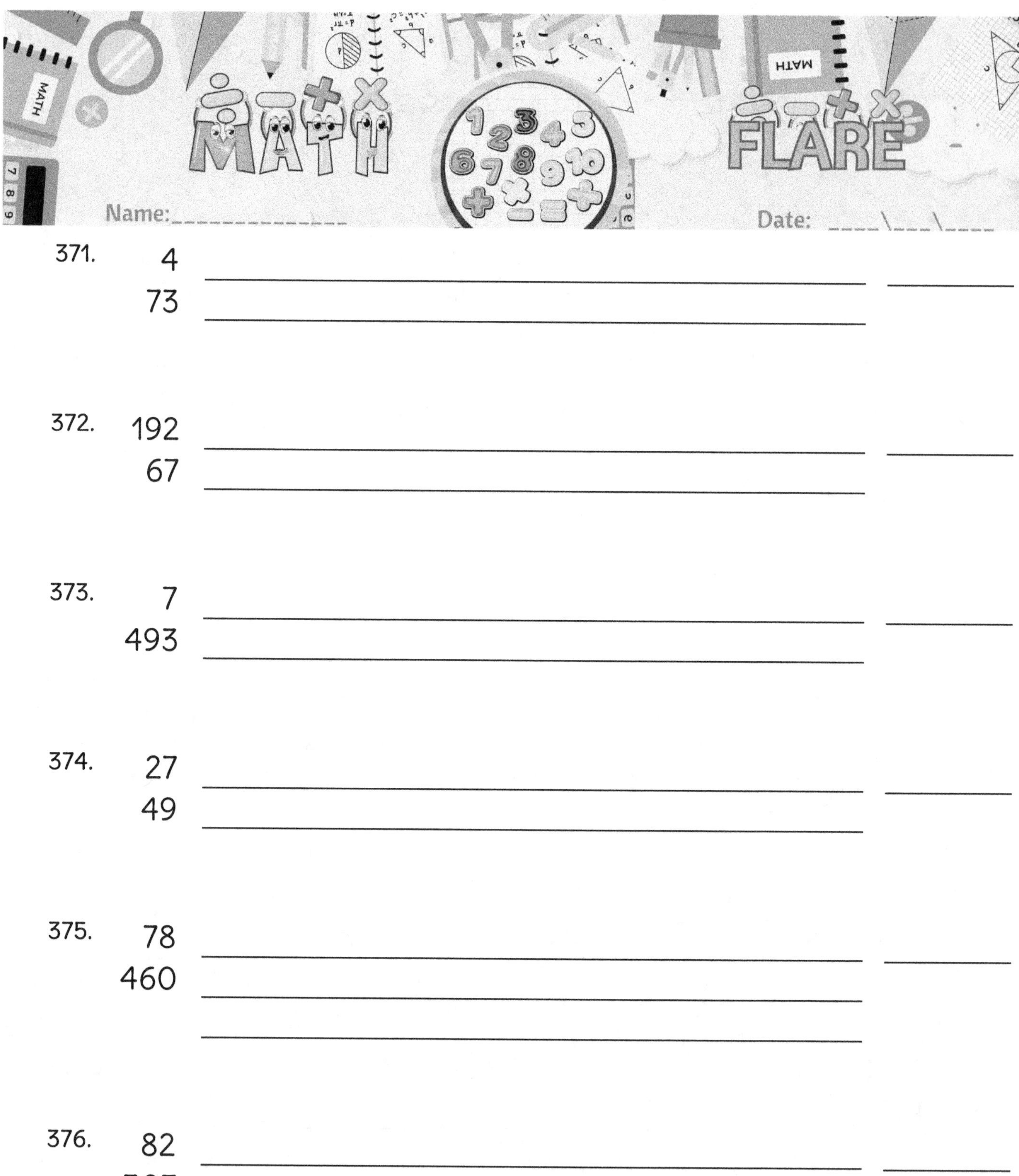

371. 4
73

372. 192
67

373. 7
493

374. 27
49

375. 78
460

376. 82
307

377. 5
      9

378. 6
      242

379. 341
      36

380. 431
      412

381. 9
      5

382. 310
      23

383. 11

      2

384. 402

      33

385. 93

      43

386. 5

      69

387. 6

      9

388. 33

      404

389. 185
     379

390. 282
     360

391. 459
     35

392. 68
     17

393. 4
     426

394. 6
     72

395. 41
      32

396. 65
      27

397. 4
      7

398. 7
      13

399. 9
      35

400. 2
      5

401.   2
     239

402.   89
     31

403.   11
     5

404.   5
     4

405.   30
     113

406.   77
     6

407. 406

      47

408.   4
       58

409.   9
        4

410. 164
      273

411. 489
        2

412.   12
      407

413.   33

      434

414.   3

      244

415.   3

      72

416.   2

      4

417.   60

      26

418.   9

      30

419. 57
      5 ____ ________

420. 108
      8 ____ ________

421. 430
      421 ____ ________

422. 82
      87 ____ ________

423. 410
      7 ____ ________

ANSWERS

Page 1: Factors

1. 7

2. 3, 7, 9, 21

3. 2, 3

4. 3, 9, 29, 87

5. 2, 4, 8

6. 2, 3, 4, 6, 8, 12, 16, 24

7. 3, 17

8. 3, 9

9. None

10. None

11. 3, 31

12. 2, 3, 4, 6, 8, 9, 12, 16, 18, 24, 27, 36, 48, 54, 72, 108, 144, 216

13. None

14. None

15. 2, 4, 8, 16, 32

16. 2

17. 5, 19

18. 7, 41

19. 2, 7

20. None

21. None

22. 2, 5

23. 2, 4

24. 3

25. 2, 137

26. 3, 107

27. None

28. None

29. 19, 23

30. 3, 9, 13, 39

31. 2, 3, 6, 9, 18, 19, 38, 57, 114, 171

32. 2, 3, 4, 6, 8, 12

33. 2, 4, 7, 8, 14, 28, 49, 56, 98, 196

34. 2, 11

35. None

36. 3, 5, 11, 15, 33, 55

37. None

38. 3, 37

39. 2, 3, 4, 5, 6, 10, 12, 15, 20, 30

40. 3, 9, 11, 33

41. 2, 151

42. 2, 5, 7, 10, 14, 35, 49, 70, 98, 245

43. 2, 4, 5, 10

44. None

45. None

46. 2, 3, 4, 6, 12, 19, 38, 57, 76, 114

47. None

48. 3, 101

49. 3, 5, 7, 9, 15, 21, 35, 45, 63, 105

50. 2, 3, 4, 6, 9, 11, 12, 18, 22, 33, 36, 44, 66, 99, 132, 198

51. 2, 19

52. 2, 3, 4, 6

53. 2, 3, 4, 6, 8, 9, 12, 18, 24, 36

54. None

55. 5, 53

56. 2, 3, 5, 6, 10, 11, 15, 22, 30, 33, 55, 66, 110, 165

57. 2, 3, 4, 6, 8, 12, 16, 24, 32, 48, 64, 96

58. 2, 233

59. None

60. 2, 3, 6, 9, 18, 27

61. 2, 4, 5, 10, 20, 25, 50

62. 2, 7, 14, 17, 34, 119

63. 3, 103

64. 2, 23

65. 2, 5, 10, 25, 50, 125

66. 2, 11, 17, 22, 34, 187

67. 2, 11, 22, 121

68. 2, 3, 6, 43, 86, 129

69. 2, 4, 8, 47, 94, 188

70. 2, 43

71. 3, 19

72. 2, 3, 4, 6, 11, 12, 22, 33, 44, 66

73. 2, 3, 6, 7, 9, 14, 18, 21, 27, 42, 54, 63, 126, 189

74. 3, 23

75. 2, 167

76. 2, 3, 4, 6, 7, 8, 12, 14, 21, 24, 28, 42, 56, 84

77. 2, 41

78. 7, 59

79. 2, 4, 23, 46

80. 2, 3, 6, 23, 46, 69

Page 11: Prime Numbers

81. 1 (No)

82. 2×2×2 (No)

83. 5×13 (No)

84. 13×17 (No)

85. 19 (Yes)

86. 7 (Yes)

87. 2×2×2×2×2×2×3 (No)

88. 5×7 (No)

89. 5×29 (No)

90. 2×2×5×5×5 (No)

91. 2×3×3×5 (No)

92. 2×2×11 (No)

93. 3×3 (No)

94. 2×227 (No)

95. 2×41 (No)

96. 11×17 (No)

97. 2×2×7×7 (No)

98. 3×3×3×3 (No)

99. 2×2×2×2×13 (No)

100. 2×2 (No)

101. 3×11 (No)

102. 443 (Yes)

103. 2×3×3 (No)

104. 5 (Yes)

105. 3×7×7 (No)

106. 3 (Yes)

107. 2×5×31 (No)

108. 2×3 (No)

109. 2 (Yes)

110. 2×3×7 (No)

111. 59 (Yes)

112. 3×5×5×5 (No)

113. 2×3×3×11 (No)

114. 179 (Yes)

115. 3×7×13 (No)

116. 2×29 (No)

117. 347 (Yes)

118. 3×29 (No)

119. 2×107 (No)

120. 3×3×3 (No)

121. 61 (Yes)

122. 2×2×2×2×2×2×5 (No)

123. 2×13×19 (No)

124. 5×5×17 (No)

125. 2×2×97 (No)

126. 2×47 (No)

127. 2×2×17 (No)

128. 5×19 (No)

129. 3×5×7 (No)

130. 31 (Yes)

131. 2×2×83 (No)

132. 2×2×73 (No)

133. 2×2×2×7 (No)

134. 2×5×5 (No)

135. 2×149 (No)

136. 2×2×7 (No)

137. 3×7×17 (No)

138. 2×2×2×2×2×2 (No)

139. 2×71 (No)

140. 2×3×17 (No)

141. 3×31 (No)

142. 3×3×5×7 (No)

143. 2×2×5×19 (No)

144. 23 (Yes)

145. 7×7 (No)

146. 2×2×23 (No)

147. 2×31 (No)

148. 11×31 (No)

149. 89 (Yes)

150. 5×5 (No)

151. 13 (Yes)

152. 2×5×5×7 (No)

153. 11×23 (No)

154. 2×2×2×7×7 (No)

155. 3×23 (No)

156. 2×2×2×41 (No)

157. 2×199 (No)

158. 269 (Yes)

Page 16: Greatest Common Factor

159. 36	160. 2	161. 2	162. 4	163. 14	164. 15	165. 2
166. 11	167. 5	168. 5	169. 22	170. 21	171. 7	172. 22
173. 25	174. 7	175. 11	176. 6	177. 5	178. 6	179. 3
180. 2	181. 63	182. 14	183. 15	184. 5	185. 3	186. 126
187. 2	188. 22	189. 8	190. 5	191. 4	192. 8	193. 2
194. 2	195. 4	196. 5	197. 5	198. 2	199. 90	200. 66

201. 5   202. 4   203. 3   204. 2   205. 30   206. 3   207. 2

208. 6   209. 5   210. 2   211. 33   212. 7   213. 11   214. 3

215. 8   216. 2   217. 33   218. 2   219. 5   220. 2   221. 11

222. 2   223. 11   224. 7   225. 14   226. 7   227. 4   228. 11

229. 115   230. 5   231. 11   232. 3   233. 49   234. 11   235. 7

Page 29: Multiples

236. 2, 4, 6, 8, 10

237. 233, 466, 699, 932, 1,165

238. 1, 2, 3, 4, 5

239. 200, 400, 600, 800, 1,000

240. 97, 194, 291, 388, 485

241. 9, 18, 27, 36, 45

242. 76, 152, 228, 304, 380

243. 46, 92, 138, 184, 230

244. 397, 794, 1,191, 1,588, 1,985

245. 50, 100, 150, 200, 250

246. 12, 24, 36, 48, 60

247. 7, 14, 21, 28, 35

248. 17, 34, 51, 68, 85

249. 4, 8, 12, 16, 20

250. 56, 112, 168, 224, 280

251. 45, 90, 135, 180, 225

252. 89, 178, 267, 356, 445

253. 20, 40, 60, 80, 100

254. 72, 144, 216, 288, 360

255. 3, 6, 9, 12, 15

256. 77, 154, 231, 308, 385

257. 432, 864, 1,296, 1,728, 2,160

258. 236, 472, 708, 944, 1,180

259. 98, 196, 294, 392, 490

260. 323, 646, 969, 1,292, 1,615

261. 383, 766, 1,149, 1,532, 1,915

262. 152, 304, 456, 608, 760

263. 95, 190, 285, 380, 475

264. 219, 438, 657, 876, 1,095

265. 8, 16, 24, 32, 40

266. 108, 216, 324, 432, 540

267. 265, 530, 795, 1,060, 1,325

268. 37, 74, 111, 148, 185

269. 444, 888, 1,332, 1,776, 2,220

270. 55, 110, 165, 220, 275

271. 73, 146, 219, 292, 365

272. 297, 594, 891, 1,188, 1,485

273. 83, 166, 249, 332, 415

274. 440, 880, 1,320, 1,760, 2,200

275. 47, 94, 141, 188, 235

276. 415, 830, 1,245, 1,660, 2,075

277. 346, 692, 1,038, 1,384, 1,730

278. 304, 608, 912, 1,216, 1,520

279. 64, 128, 192, 256, 320

280. 214, 428, 642, 856, 1,070

281. 28, 56, 84, 112, 140

282. 482, 964, 1,446, 1,928, 2,410

283. 121, 242, 363, 484, 605

284. 79, 158, 237, 316, 395

285. 14, 28, 42, 56, 70

286. 368, 736, 1,104, 1,472, 1,840

287. 164, 328, 492, 656, 820

288. 388, 776, 1,164, 1,552, 1,940

289. 62, 124, 186, 248, 310

290. 361, 722, 1,083, 1,444, 1,805

291. 22, 44, 66, 88, 110

292. 500, 1,000, 1,500, 2,000, 2,500

293. 96, 192, 288, 384, 480

294. 80, 160, 240, 320, 400

295. 29, 58, 87, 116, 145

296. 30, 60, 90, 120, 150

297. 88, 176, 264, 352, 440

298. 5, 10, 15, 20, 25

299. 422, 844, 1,266, 1,688, 2,110

300. 6, 12, 18, 24, 30

301. 67, 134, 201, 268, 335

302. 183, 366, 549, 732, 915

303. 36, 72, 108, 144, 180

304. 171, 342, 513, 684, 855

305. 60, 120, 180, 240, 300

306. 172, 344, 516, 688, 860

307. 353, 706, 1,059, 1,412, 1,765

308. 41, 82, 123, 164, 205

309. 364, 728, 1,092, 1,456, 1,820

310. 293, 586, 879, 1,172, 1,465

311. 54, 108, 162, 216, 270

312. 33, 66, 99, 132, 165

313. 457, 914, 1,371, 1,828, 2,285

314. 499, 998, 1,497, 1,996, 2,495

315. 400, 800, 1,200, 1,600, 2,000

316. 366, 732, 1,098, 1,464, 1,830

317. 487, 974, 1,461, 1,948, 2,435

318. 266, 532, 798, 1,064, 1,330

319. 90, 180, 270, 360, 450

320. 403, 806, 1,209, 1,612, 2,015

321. 21, 42, 63, 84, 105

322. 85, 170, 255, 340, 425

323. 426, 852, 1,278, 1,704, 2,130

324. 63, 126, 189, 252, 315

325. 132, 264, 396, 528, 660

326. 365, 730, 1,095, 1,460, 1,825

327. 27, 54, 81, 108, 135

328. 39, 78, 117, 156, 195

329. 386, 772, 1,158, 1,544, 1,930

330. 138, 276, 414, 552, 690

Page 41: Lowest Common Multiple

331. 1,263	332. 696	333. 111	334. 3,519	335. 2,170
336. 51	337. 37,920	338. 228	339. 69,774	340. 9
341. 172	342. 174	343. 3,008	344. 2,938	345. 3,298

346. 288   347. 24   348. 66   349. 99   350. 580

351. 162   352. 3,744   353. 497   354. 18,582   355. 24

356. 4,620   357. 14   358. 1,749   359. 132   360. 900

361. 20   362. 14,210   363. 315   364. 2,035   365. 65

366. 1,040   367. 150   368. 182   369. 803   370. 22,540

371. 292   372. 12,864   373. 3,451   374. 1,323   375. 17,940

376. 25,174   377. 45   378. 726   379. 12,276   380. 177,572

381. 45   382. 7,130   383. 22   384. 4,422   385. 3,999

386. 345   387. 18   388. 13,332   389. 70,115   390. 16,920

391. 16,065   392. 68   393. 852   394. 72   395. 1,312

396. 1,755   397. 28   398. 91   399. 315   400. 10

401. 478   402. 2,759   403. 55   404. 20   405. 3,390

406. 462   407. 19,082   408. 116   409. 36   410. 44,772

411. 978   412. 4,884   413. 14,322   414. 732   415. 72

416. 4   417. 780   418. 90   419. 285   420. 216

421. 181,030   422. 7,134   423. 2,870